X Drama Queen

RECOVERED FROM TRAUMA

Dr. April Griseta

TRILOGY CHRISTIAN PUBLISHERS
TUSTIN, CA

Trilogy Christian Publishers
A Wholly Owned Subsidiary of Trinity Broadcasting Network
2442 Michelle Drive
Tustin, CA 92780

10 9 8 7 6 5 4 3 2 1

Library of Congress Cataloging-in-Publication Data is available.

ISBN 978-1-63769-230-1

ISBN 978-1-63769-231-8 (ebook)

Contents

Dedication

This book is lovingly dedicated to my husband, Joseph. My best friend has patiently sat by while I spent numerous hours studying, typing, and editing manuscripts, completing sermons, and assisting my daughter with her three children. He has denied his own needs to sacrifice for others. To him, I am eternally grateful.

Message from the Author

Sometimes when reading very sensitive material, or material that reminds you of your past, negative emotions can get stirred up. You may start to feel anxious, depressed, or angry. This means that some further healing needs to come to you. Please seek out a counselor and receive help. There is no shame in seeking help. In fact, it is to be commended. It means you want to be made whole and no longer tormented by your past.

While this is not a medical book on how the brain stores traumatic memories, it will touch on how you may have suppressed traumatic memories and still get triggered today by environmental cues. Understanding what may be happening to you is empowering and helps normalize your experience. You are not alone and there are many community resources available. Psychoeducational support groups with Christ at the center are highly recommended for healing (if not contraindicated). By this I mean some highly traumatized people are not ready for a group experience and may need individual counseling first.

It is truly my hope that X Drama Queen will bring some revelatory insight and begin to facilitate healing. God wants to restore health to you and heal you of your wounds (Jeremiah 30:17). This has been my personal Scripture that has carried me through some very difficult times. Ask God for yours.

Introduction

There are many reasons drama queens exist. Some are desperately seeking attention; others enjoy the chaos of battle; and yet others just love sharing their misery. All of us may have encountered this queen who thrives on turmoil. She can be highly theatrical and perceive other people's problems as always less severe than hers. But what has helped create the drama queen?

Somewhere a deep inner need has not been met or these behaviors may have been learned and reinforced by the attention it brings them. Turmoil may be a familiar environment or maybe traumatophilia (attraction and fascination to trauma and danger) has developed. Many of the drama queens that I have met have suffered from some sort of abuse, neglect, or abandonment during childhood. Their childhood dependency needs (love, attention) have not been met by primary caregivers and they continually search for this need to be filled.

Their cry is heard far into adulthood. It can be quite irksome and does not seem age-appropriate. The poor soul continually cries, "Somebody pay attention to me." Some will even create battles just to be noticed. They feel that some negative attention is better than being ignored or rejected.

Unfortunately, many drama queens sabotage themselves, as people start to move away from them instead of giving them the attention they crave. Some have met diagnostic criteria or at least some traits that fit the Cluster B personality disorders (such as narcissistic personality disorder, borderline personality disorder, and histrionic personality disorder) and others may have met the criteria for other mental health disorders. A clinician would have to make a full assessment to give a proper diagnosis (if any) but drama queens for the most part are self-absorbed, emotionally unstable, and very theatrical in their presentation.

Past trauma may have caused fragmentation of self or boundary difficulties, nevertheless one can choose to continually live a life of drama through trauma repetition and reenactments, or one can choose to surrender to the Lordship of Christ. One may also choose to continually be triggered by past pain and have bouts of confusion or one may choose to take the necessary steps leading toward wholeness.

X Drama Queen will look at the impact of various trauma, saboteurs and the faulty ways drama queens have used to cope and or manipulate. The book, however, does not stop there but delightfully leads to the place of overcoming. As you read through the pages one can learn how to navigate crisis, make better choices, and dismantle psychological defenses that no longer work. If you are the drama queen or know of one, this book will bring insight into the world where she lives; and how she attempts to rule and reign.

1

Trauma and Drama

For God is not the author of confusion *but* of peace.

1 Corinthians 14:33, NKJV

Moths Around the Flame

Trauma can help create repetitive drama. Victims of trauma have been known to recreate scenarios that are familiar to their past. They start fires and camp around the flame. Did you know that the drama queen may simply be reenacting past trauma to finally gain mastery over fear or to feel some sort of control? "Trauma repetition is an effort by victims to bring resolution to a traumatic memory. By repeating the experience, the victims try anew to figure out a way to respond to eliminate fear."[1]

Also, if there is no drama around, they feel that something is wrong and will create a disturbance or some sort of sick excitement. She says, "I can feel something now, I am no longer numb." Past trauma may have caused a shut down of feelings. Drama in my own life has at times relieved psychological pain, temporarily. I am not saying I wanted to feel pain, but I am saying I wanted to feel alive. As distorted as it may sound, chaos helped "ground" me to a reality I was very comfortable with.

Some drama queens are so hungry for attention, they will "act out" to get it. While this term is often used for unruly children it applies to the drama queen as well. According to *Healthline*, "Acting out behavior is when one exhibits unrestrained and improper actions. The behavior is usually caused by suppressed or denied feelings or emotions. Acting out is a way to seek attention and a desire for power. Acting out allows them to feel in control over their actions."[2]

Many people have experienced trauma in their lives. Some continually have night terrors, panic attacks, and floating anxiety. Yet others suffer little. Of course, many factors contribute to this such as duration of adverse events, age at the time of trauma, severity, "characteristics of the individual, developmental processes and sociocultural factors."[3] Also, of critical importance is "the meaning that the survivor has attached to the traumatic experience."[4] "Traumas perceived as intentionally harmful often make the event more traumatic for people and communities."⁵ Victims of trauma can suffer greatly and may need tools to build resilience.

Trauma is an interesting animal and hard to define because what trauma is for one person may not be trauma for another and the impact of a particular trauma may not visit until many years later when the victim is triggered. Certain triggers or environmental cues (smells, anniversaries, particular locations) may awaken suppressed traumatic memories.

An example of this is one day I was in the shower and started to panic for no apparent reason. Later I learned that a suppressed memory of childhood sexual abuse (that happened to me in a bathroom) was awakened. When something bad happens, our minds want to suppress that memory, especially if the event was emotionally charged or physical pain was involved.

For simplicity, we can say trauma is an event that overwhelmed you and created some type of internal response (such as horror or helplessness). Your physical and psychological integrity may have been threatened and you were greatly impacted. As a result of that traumatic experience, some sort of alteration happened.

Some of the effects of trauma may be the changing or altering of one's feelings toward God and others. Author Judith Herman remarks, "traumatized people lose their trust in themselves, in other people and in God."⁶

Mistrust is very common, along with the fear of intimacy. In later chapters, I will discuss attachment injuries. Some trauma-impacted persons may question the love of God and have difficulty with faith. They may also have difficulty with how they view themselves after a traumatic event. Many in the body of Christ suffer from low self-worth and see themselves as "damaged goods" due to past trauma. Ronnie Janoff-Bulman notes, "traumatic events frequently challenge one's core about safety, self-worth and the meaning of life."[7]

Often, victims of trauma pick bad mates, or the wolves find them, as they smell the bleeding of the trauma. They somehow seem to pick up on the scent of vulnerability. Revictimization is often seen.

"Damaged Goods" Perception

People in the Bible thought they were damaged goods or not good enough for anything. Moses did not think he could speak for God due to his speech problem (Exodus 4:10). Gideon said he was the weakest in the clan (Judges 6:15), and Saul hid behind the equipment (1 Samuel 10:22). But through God's strength they were victorious.

People who suffer from trauma may shut down all feelings, may be unable to have loving feelings, or may blame themselves for the trauma to gain some sort of mastery over what has happened to them. This is called locus of control. Yet others may be chronically depressed or blame others and stew in a bitter pool. Like I said earlier, trauma affects people differently. The effects of trauma may cause people to overreact to a situation that reminds them of a past trauma. That reaction may seem "overdramatic" to onlookers. The onlookers may even say, "what a drama queen" and leave their presence scratching their heads wondering, "What just happened?" Guess what? The drama queen may be just as perplexed. Author Enod Gray asserts:

> Memories of trauma stay stuck in the nether regions of the brain which are not accessible by the frontal lobes-the thinking conscious part of the brain. Do you ever overreact or feel weird about a situation without understanding why you feel so upset or abandoned or out of control? If so, it is likely that you have called up a feeling from the unconscious part of your brain because the present situation is similar in some way to the traumatic situation in your past. The current situation has unconsciously triggered a reaction to past trauma.[8]

People who have experienced trauma may have delayed reactions. Some emotional reactions may be irritability and/or hostility, mood swings, depression, anxiety, and emotional detachment. Some delayed behavioral responses may be social relationship disturbances, engagement in high-risk situations, and increased use of alcohol or drugs. Delayed cognitive responses may include difficulty making decisions and belief that feelings are dangerous.[9] While this list is not all-inclusive, it is a starting point to look at the impact of trauma.

Trauma can be crippling, as will be seen as we look at the biblical account (found in 2 Samuel 9:1-13) of the portrayal of a man named Mephibosheth. He was dropped by his nurse and ended up with lame feet as a child. Many of us have been dropped by someone along the way. Someone who was supposed to take care of you failed. It crippled you. Perhaps someone in your life dropped the ball and it left you lame or stuck in a dry place. Mephibosheth ended up living in Lodibar, a desert, a dry place. The good news is that he did not stay there, as someone gave him support.

As the story goes, King David looked to show kindness to the house of Saul and Mephibosheth happened to be Saul's grandson. So, one day the King calls for Mephibosheth and he ends up eating at the King's table and receiving a royal pension for the rest of his life. We should never underestimate the power of support.

This story is likened to that of Christ who picks us up in our despair and makes us a royal priesthood and part of His family. He bore our shame on the cross. Interestingly, Mephibosheth's name means shame. But he would have shame no more. God brought him from tragedy to triumph; from tears to turn around.

People with unhealed trauma often carry chaos wherever they go. I call them chaos carriers. I understand this well, as I used to be a chaos carrier. I would pick fights with my husband to get a rise out of him because peace was boring and uneventful. But because my husband is a man of God he would not engage in contention. After a while, I began to enjoy peace. Now I get very disturbed if something comes in to disturb my peace. Healing has come to me. I am no longer a drama queen.

Remember when people overreact it is usually out of a place of unresolved pain or past trauma. Many deny the pain and many mask the pain but the pain will eventually leak. It will leak in sarcasm, criticism, bitter water, grumbling, and even gallows humor (hurt the person and say, "just joking"). The drama queen may be manifesting.

Questions to Consider:

1. Have you ever had a traumatic event happen to you?
2. How did you react immediately after it happened?
3. Did you have a delayed response?
4. Is peace boring?
5. Do you see yourself as damaged goods?
6. Do you carry shame and guilt?
7. Do you like to be around strife and contention?
8. Do you find yourself attracted to turmoil? Why do you think that is?
9. Do you have trouble setting boundaries with people?
10. Do you have trouble telling people no?
11. Do you want to control everybody and all circumstances?
12. Do you always want to be the center of attention?
13. Has there been a pattern of tumultuous relationships?

2

The Trauma of Childhood Sexual Abuse

For I will restore health to you and heal you of
your wounds, says the Lord.
Jeremiah 30:17, NKJV

I was a victim of severe child sexual abuse. After all the violence, I was no longer me. I was a happy-go-lucky kid one day and the next an ashamed, withdrawn, compliant child. People have asked, "why you did not tell anyone until later in life?" This is a good question. First, my mother witnessed the rape and knew about the abuse. She had the abuser removed from the home and nothing was ever said after that. This led me to believe I had done something wrong and the words, "what did I do wrong?" still ring in my head today.

Christian Sanderson, author of *Counseling Adult Survivors of Sexual Abuse*, sheds some great insight on the dynamics of Childhood Sexual Abuse (CSA). She points out:

> A long-term effect of CSA is the shattering of self. Child sexual abuse in a very young child may prevent the development of a unified self, which can lead to an absent or fragmented sense of self. For healthy development, it is crucial to have a unified sense of self. Survivors of CSA often feel fragmented and split and the sense of self-worth is destroyed. This results in alienation from the self and others and a sense of being a psychological orphan. Some adult survivors of CSA may compensate for this shattering of the self by becoming self-absorbed and narcissistic.[10]

I remember always feeling somewhat detached or weird, peculiar, and cast away after the event. I also remember always looking for approval and acceptance. I honestly believed no one would ever want me and found myself involved with people that agreed with my assertion.

Many adult survivors of CSA become addicted to pain and struggle for survival as this may be all they have ever known and thus hard to relinquish. The adult survivor may be able to see himself [or herself] only as a sexual object, with his [or her] sexuality being his own only value. They may become oversexualized and develop sexual preoccupation and compulsions including compulsive masturbations. In contrast they may have an aversion to sexual intimacy.[11]

The good news is God can restore the brokenness and give a healthy identity in Him. God can bring wholeness. He can also deliver people from compulsivity.

Many of the behavioral effects commonly seen in adult survivors of CSA can be understood within the context of the repetition of traumatic behaviors they have experienced. Trauma can lead to traumatophilia (an attraction and fascination with trauma and danger) resembling the survivor's inner trauma experiences.[12]

The Abuser

Child abusers get remarkably close to the family and the victim and become a trusted friend. Once they commit the act of violence, a violation of trust has occurred. The child will often take all the blame in silence. There is a silence that can be heard and a darkness that can be felt. In my case, "it" was never talked about. In many cases, nothing is ever said. The abuser "grooms" the child in such a way, their special secret is never exposed.

> In CSA, the child effectively loses both parents, the sexually abusive parent in terms of being caring and nurtured and the non-abusing parent in the child's need to protect in avoiding closeness for fear of inadvertently disclosing the CSA. In many cases, the abuser capitalizes on this by deliberately driving a wedge between the non-abusing parent and the child as a form of insurance that the child is less likely to disclose.[13]

"The need to protect the family is a common reaction to CSA because the child is dependent on the family for survival."[14] Kids are afraid to be left all alone.

The child really does not want to lose the one who has been playing with her/him. The abuser becomes their friend or playmate. The abuser may play on this to decrease the risk of being exposed. You see, my friend would play games with me and give me quarters in my ring dings. I felt so loved. After all, he played cards and jacks with me. This is particularly heinous because it plays on the innocence of the child.

In my case, not only did I lose my supposed special friend, but my mother also withdrew into herself as she witnessed the event. So, I lost my mother too. She was gagged and tied to a toilet. She was forced to watch and utterly helpless. Afterward, she was so riddled with guilt and shame she began to drink heavily and did not stop drinking. Not a word was spoken, and I felt like I must have been a bad girl, I must have done something wrong. These feelings carried over into adult life.

The enemy wanted to silence me at an early age. The enemy likes to go after the young. We see this in the Bible how Pharaoh wanted the children killed right on the birthing stool and Herod wanted all children under the age of two slaughtered. The enemy is after "seed".

If a child comes and tells you they have been sexually violated, please do not discount what they are saying. It took a lot of courage to come and tell you. Take the claim seriously.

Questions to Consider:

1. Did you grow up feeling safe? Why or why not?
2. Were you envious of families that seemed to have it all together?
3. Do you believe you have trust issues?
4. Do you find yourself suspicious of other people's motives?
5. How do you view God?

3

The Trauma
of Childhood
Emotional Neglect

*Behold, children are a heritage from the Lord, the fruit of the
womb is a reward. Like arrows in the hand of a warrior, so
are the children of one's youth. Happy is the man who has
his quiver full of them; they shall not be ashamed, but shall
speak with their enemies in the gate.*
Psalm 127:3-5, NKJV

Your children are a gift from the Lord. I know sometimes it may not feel like that when they give you a
whole lot of trouble. But they truly are a gift. They are a
priceless legacy bequeathed to us. They are like arrows
in the hand of a warrior and happy is the man who has a
quiver full of them. Arrows are an arsenal! So, Scripture
says children are a gift and happy is the man who has a

lot of them, so, there is obviously something very wrong if a child is neglected and not treasured.

Let us face it, many of us have been neglected or ignored by our parents at some time in our lives. Perhaps they were overworked, tired, or distracted but I am talking about a pervasive pattern of neglect between caregiver and child. Childhood emotional neglect is extremely detrimental to children in many ways but let us first get a good working definition.

> Children who have had been emotionally neglected have been hurt by either the parent failed them in some way in a moment of crises causing a very severe wound (acute empathetic failure) or the parent was "tone deaf" to some aspect of a child's need through their development (chronic empathetic failure). It may have been both.[15]

We know that harsh, demeaning words hurt children, but a lack of encouragement hurts too.

> Emotionally neglected children have been denied what they need to develop feelings. As adults they find they lack the ability to call up and name what they are feeling. It is not that the feelings are not there, they have been

repressed in the service of survival from the
unbearable truth of not feeling love. Love is
the root need of all human beings.[16]

Just imagine always feeling alone in this scary world.
Children who grow up in drug-addicted homes or have
parents who are depressed or ill often feel this way. I
remember as a child escaping into schoolwork. I am
fifty-eight and still in some sort of continuous study. I
remember always feeling lonely.

Children in an effort to cope with loneliness
learn to put other people's needs first as the
price of admission to a relationship. They are
also eager to leave their childhood behind and
grow up quickly. They are competent beyond
their years but lonely to the core.[17]

I remember in the second grade I was reading at an
eighth-grade reading level. As I grew older, everyone's
needs were always placed before mine. They just always
seemed to be more important. I always felt like I was
bothering people if I made any needs known.

When these children grow up, they expect the
same treatment from others that their parents gave them, they lack confidence, they are

convinced they would be bothering others if
they made their needs known.[18]

I had to start playing a different tape. I had to start
declaring what God's Word said about me. Listed below
is a list of positive declarations:

- I am deeply loved by Father. I ravish His
  heart. I am on His mind. His thoughts of me
  are innumerous.
- I am a special hidden treasure and the apple
  of His eye.
- He cares for me greatly and His loving kindness knows no end.
- He desires to do me good and give me a future and a hope.
- God is on my side.
- I am a friend of God.

Questions to Consider:

1. Did you feel like you were a gift?
2. If you were neglected, how did you cope?
3. Do you find yourself using the same coping mechanisms today?
4. Do you sense a "neediness" about yourself?
5. Do you escape into books or fantasy?

4

The Trauma of Mean or Unavailable Mommies

For she leaves her eggs on the ground, and warms them in the dust; she forgets that a foot may crush them, or that a wild beast may break them. She treats her young harshly, as though they were not hers; her labor is in vain, without concern.

Job 39:14-16, NKJV

While there are many reasons a mother may not nurture her child, the effects of this behavior can be long lasting on the child. Peg Streep, author of *Daughter Detox*, states that children who are not shown maternal love believe they are unlovable, believe it is their fault, and search for a sense of belonging their entire lives.[19]

I was never genuinely hugged by my mother or ever told I was loved. My brother was somewhat disabled, so much of the attention went to him. Boys were the ones who got pampered in the family and the women were to be strong and independent. As a child, all I remember was a profound sense of loneliness and sadness. I also remember, however, that same sadness and loneliness on my mother. Her brother was favored, and her mother was hyper-critical of her. Generational patterns can be seen here. With that said, the lack of nurturing may have been learned behavior. Jonice Webb, author of *Running on Empty*, speaks of passing the emotional torch of neglect and informs her readers that emotional neglect is invisible and easily passes from generation to generation.[20]

The Bible tells of a day where people would have no natural affection (2 Timothy 3:3). As the days grow eviler, people will become more self-absorbed. We then can suppose that children will only be a hindrance, as caregiving requires sacrifice.

Mothers who suffer from depression (or have other mental health disorders) and various medical illnesses may not have any emotional or physical energy to invest in their children. The child does not know this, he or she only feels neglected and unloved. Also, many abused women do not have the emotional wherewithal to deal with caregiving.

Many single mothers must work two jobs and when they come home, they are exhausted. Community help may be beneficial but cannot replace Mom's nurturing. Father absenteeism exacerbates the issue.

Attachment Injury

An attachment injury is, "being hurt by someone who is supposed to be there for you, someone like a parent, grandparent, spouse, someone you are attached to as your caregiver, or other loved one. Attachment injuries occur when in times of stress, we expect a loved one to be there for us, and for whatever reason he or she is not."[21]

This causes a great deal of pain and can have lasting negative effects. "Such injuries can ignite life's core pains: anger, anxiety, fear, grief and suffering of various kinds."[22] The good news is there is help there, but the bad news is it can become costly to treat. This is a topic worthy of further research and hopefully grant funding.

Questions to Consider:

1. Has someone dropped the ball in your life?
2. What kind of feelings did you harbor as a child?
3. Is a sense of loneliness prevalent in your life today?
4. Are you easily enraged?
5. Do you have difficulty receiving love?
6. Do you have difficulty identifying your feelings?

5

Various Reactions to Pain

*Behold, I will bring it health and healing; I will heal them
and reveal to them the abundance of peace and truth.*
Jeremiah 33:6, NKJV

People often react out of their own unresolved pain
and look to defend themselves. Sometimes the defense
looks exaggerated, mean, or even weird. You will find
the drama queen in the midst of the following defenses.

The animal kingdom can give us great insight into
defenses. The bull in the china shop will steamroll over
you and bust up everything around him. They do not
care who gets hurt in the process. Then afterward, they
will act like nothing happened. I can almost guarantee
they learned this way to resolve conflict growing up.
Some parents have role-modeled bad behavior. Now we
have children who are adults but still acting like chil-

dren. We have adults with temper tantrums and spiritual hissy fits.

The turtle hides his head in his shell and will stick out his head when it feels safe to do so. It runs from all conflict. People who run from conflict often become angry because their own needs are unmet.

The porcupine quills injure. I liken this to the one who brings up every mistake you have ever made. It is an attempt to disable you and make you feel bad about yourself.

Now let us look at the viper who injects venom. This can be likened to a person who uses his mouth (fangs) to inflict pain on others. It is a poisonous concoction which looks to kill by ruining someone's reputation.

The scorpion also uses venom. One night on my way to church, I saw a van with a huge scorpion decal. I knew the Lord was highlighting it to me. When I got to church, I got attacked by a congregant. This person attacked my identity as a Pastor. I was left stunned and stung.

The last animal I will talk about is the skunk. His only real defense is his noxious smell. These are like the people who are always complaining about some supposed injustice done to them. Unforgiveness has a certain smell.

In the professional field of counseling, these are called defenses which all look to self-preserve but never deal with the problem. As humans we can become very sophisticated in defending ourselves, we tend to rehearse injustices and continually spar in our heads to beat our opponent. The funny thing is, he or she is not even listening and probably could not even care that you have been hurt. You may play in your head all the winning scenarios or the things you should have said to let them really *have it*.

You may take revenge, which is sad because it does not leave room for God to avenge, or you may simply take your marbles and go home. Sometimes, people blame others for everything and even blame God for their plight. However, since the days of old, humans are still looking to transfer blame. It seems that most often we do not want to own up but perhaps things are being revealed to be healed.

We need to look through the lens of Calvary and remember how much we have been forgiven. I often think God allows things to happen in our lives to show us what is in our own hearts. The heart can be desperately wicked (see Jeremiah 17:9).

"If it is possible, as much as depends on you, live peaceably with all men" (Romans 12:18, NKJV). This is said because some people do not want peace, as their narrative is more suitable for their purposes or more entertaining to their flesh. Why believe the truth when a lie may be more exciting?

Going Deeper with Defenses

> Behold, you desire truth in the inward parts,
> and in the hidden part You will make me to
> know wisdom.
>
> Psalm 51:6, NKJV

Many people use psychological defense mechanisms to evade pain. It is important to look at entrenched defenses because "they may prevent us from accessing important emotions we need to face."[23] They can keep us from living the abundant life Christ has promised. It is the truth one knows that sets them free.

The concept of defenses was birthed from Sigmund Freud. "According to Freud, sometimes when people are confronted with an idea or feeling they find too painful or morally unacceptable, they ward it off and push it into the unconscious."[24] He utilized the term resistance. "If we originally warded off feelings or facts too painful to bear–that is, resorted to a defense mechanism–we will naturally resist anything that threatens to revive that pain."[25] Sometimes defense mechanisms help us get by when facing truth would be unbearable.

Many different types of defenses may be erected. Sometimes people repress hurtful memories (stuff them in the unconscious) and yet other times they may simply deny their pain.

My brother was sick for many years and I had to carry that burden. It became part of my life. Only after he died, the Lord told me He ended my suffering. I did not even realize I was suffering, as I had stuffed those feelings down. I would not allow myself to feel sadness or even anger.

Another common defense is projection. This is when people project the unwanted pieces of themselves to others. If they feel ignorant about themselves, they will say it is the other person who is stupid.

There are many other defenses such as rationalization, splitting, idealization, reaction formation, and displacement.[26] I know many people get lost in their heads rather than feel the pain in their hearts and I know many people who take out or display their anger on others. The problem here is that truth in the inward parts is not being addressed. Avoiding pain does not make it go away.

It is time to lay the ax to the root rather than only deal with the fruit (symptoms). If you can get to the root, the ugly thing will not grow back and continually affect your life. Defense mechanisms are band-aids. God wants to heal you of all your wounds.

Questions to Consider:

1. Which animal do you resemble most?
2. Do you rehearse injustices in your head?
3. Do you find yourself transferring blame rather than owning up to your responsibility?
4. Do you fantasize or get lost in movies or books?
5. How have you stuffed emotions?

6

Self-Sabotage

Hypocrite! First remove the plank from your own eye,
and then you will see clearly to remove the speck
from your brother's eye.
Matthew 7:5, NKJV

The drama queen can be very narcissistic but know she may be projecting her internal shame. "People who struggle with basic shame typically rely on three common defense mechanisms in order to ward off the painful awareness of it: narcissism, blaming and contempt. Narcissism is the primary defense against (unconscious) shame. They often project their internal ugliness."[27]

In an attempt to cover the ugly, she may "idealize her public persona to ward off shame. There's an ugly shame ridden self they don't want you or anyone else to see, ever."[28] They want your attention. "They demand the interest and admiration of others because they unconsciously feel dammed, ugly and worthless."[29]

These behaviors may help the drama queen cope but it works against her. She craves attention but people do not like being around haughtiness or those who think of themselves as better than everyone else. Arrogance smells.

Defenses may have helped you cope as a child but now they are inappropriate. As a child you may have escaped into fantasy, found solace in a cookie, or felt responsible for everything. But now as an adult, you have to live in the real world, make tough decisions, and have better coping skills.

These behaviors may have helped you at one point but now are interfering with your walk with God and other relationships. God wants you to come to Him for comfort. He also wants you to look at why you may be doing the things you are doing.

Self-pity

Drama queens often wallow in self-pity to receive comfort. They learned this when they were young. Many as children welcome self-pity as soothing medicine. Author Casper McCloud says, "one of the first places we find in dealing with self-pity is a broken heart which often is the result of a broken relationship with a father or mother or both."[30]

I shared earlier on attachment injuries but know that "self-pity is extremely dangerous because it imprisons someone in self-centeredness."[31] Again we see the making of the drama queen. If that child does not have a dad in the home and has a mother who is unavailable, the child often sinks into self.

> [Forty percent] of children the western world will go to sleep in homes in which their fathers do not live. Father absence (included emotionally unavailable ones) is a current social epidemic. Individuals raised in in a father absent environment demonstrate 5x the average suicide rate, dramatically increased rates of depression and anxiety, 32 times the average rate of incarceration, substantially increased rates of substance abuse and increase in social and mental behavioral issues. Also demonstrated, decreased education levels and consistently lower average income levels. This does not address the abandonment and betrayal the child feels. Father absence in many ways steals their birthright.[32]

Along with self-pity, there is usually some negative thinking going on and maybe some ruminations (obsessive thinking). I have found that ruminating would often increase if there was no solution to a particular problem. It was a mental exercise that led only to exhaustion.

Philippians 4:6-8 is a Scripture that can greatly help if applied:

> Be anxious for nothing, but in everything by prayer and supplication, with thanksgiving, let your requests be made known to God; 7 and the peace of God, which surpasses all understanding, will guard your hearts and minds through Christ Jesus. Finally, brethren, whatever things are true, whatever things are noble, whatever things are just, whatever things are pure, whatever things are lovely, whatever things are of good report, if there is any virtue and if there is anything praiseworthy—meditate on these things.
>
> Philippians 4:6-8, NKJV

I do want to add that giving thanks and helping others will aid in getting you out of self-pity mode. Soothing can be found in God's ways. God does not want us to wallow in the mud but press forward to that which is ahead. He does not want us to find ourselves repetitively in bad relationships or looking for ungodly ways to soothe ourselves.

You may find the drama queen finds different ways to medicate her pain. Her drug of choice may be tumultuous relationships, substances, food, shopping, or even romance. She will be in a relationship with something.

Questions to Consider:

1. Do you find yourself in repetitive unhealthy relationships?
2. Do you carry shame?
3. Do you feel ugly?
4. Is self-pity soothing to you?
5. Do you perceive yourself as a victor or victim?
6. Do you get to the point of success and do something at that point to take you out of the race?
7. How are you with commitments?

7

Love Addiction

Love does not seek its own.

1 Corinthians 13:5, NKJV

Let us face it, we all want love and there is nothing dysfunctional about it. However, I am talking about the person who must always be in a relationship to feel worth and a sense of wholeness. They are also attracted to the "high" attached to being in "romantic love".

Many do not know what real love is as the world, media, and modern-day culture have defined it as lust. They say if I am physically attracted to someone, then I am in love. While physical attraction may be a starting place this does not define biblical *love*.

You may be physically attracted to Tom Cruise, but would you say you were in love with him? Notice the world has you zoom in on only physical attraction.

We must remember the world wants to sell products and design things to please the flesh. Sexy sells, enhanced beauty sells. Airbrushing, photoshopping, nip, tucks, and Botox® is the language of the day.

I have no problem if the barn needs a little painting but when it gets out of hand, we may be looking at another issue called body dysmorphic disorder (BDD). WebMD defines body dysmorphic disorder as a distinct mental disorder in which a person is preoccupied with an imagined physical defect or a minor defect that others often cannot see. As a result, people with this disorder see themselves as "ugly" and often avoid social exposure or turn to plastic surgery to try to improve their appearance.[33]

A clinician must first do a full assessment before giving a diagnosis of BDD. This is just some basic information not to be used for diagnostic purposes.

The unrenewed mind is brainwashed and programmed to think, *if it feels good, we should be able to do it.* The world is under the sway of the wicked one. The world system says it is okay to cohabitate, it is okay to kill unborn babies, and all women should be a size 0. The world system is warped and leads to self-absorption.

Biblical love is so different. Love is patient, love is kind and love seeks not its own (1 Corinthians 13:4-5). It is not about pleasing the self at all. Some people get addicted to a warped sense of love where it is about meeting their own personal needs.

Let me start with a definition of love addiction: "When one person loves another with compulsive intensity and in ways that are not to the best interest of either person. These people always seem to choose people who apparently cannot or will not love them back."[34]

Psych Central states, "love addicts core fantasy is the expectation that someone else can solve their problems, provide unconditional positive regard and take care of them. They become love addicts due to a history of abandonment from primary caregivers."[35]

I believe there is something very intense about romance and people are attracted to that powerful experience. There is an undeniable rush about it. People gain pleasurable feelings associated with being in love. Dopamine is released.

So why not keep running after love? In other words, every time I fall in love, I feel good, so I will keep doing it. A new heartthrob, a new adventure. A quest looking for the one keeps many running on the love wheel. These are called *youthful lusts*.

Psychology Today notes causes of love addiction:

Inadequate or inconsistent nurturing

Low self esteem

Absence of positive role models for committed relationship

Indoctrination of cultural images of perfect romantic love and happily ever after
endings.[36]

What has been taught or not taught will affect our
beliefs and actions. We at times make bad choices out
of ignorance or simply look to alleviate temporary pain.
Poor relational choices can cost one greatly and can impact subsequent relationships.

Experiences in our lives also put information in our
brains and help us make sense of our world. If we have
had many horrible experiences, we may see the world
as a terrible place and always perceive the glass as half-
empty, if you will. The point trying to be made is, experiences can affect our beliefs and our vision may be
distorted.

Questions to Consider:

1. Do you feel you have to be in a relationship to be whole?
2. Do you enjoy the rush of being in love only to experience crashing?
3. Do you find nice guys boring?
4. Are you attracted to unavailable men and the chase?

8

Distorted Vision

*Now when He had said these things, He cried with a loud
voice, "Lazarus, come forth!" And he who had died came out
bound hand and foot with graveclothes, and his face was
wrapped with a cloth. Jesus said to them, "Loose him,
and let him go."*
John 11:43-44, NKJV

We see in this Scripture that Jesus raises Lazarus
from the dead, but the graveclothes need to be removed. For our purposes, graveclothes are our baggage
from the past. We cannot carry past baggage into the
next season.

Graveclothes hinder your mobility and will keep you
stuck. Graveclothes also affect your vision. You may
have a warped view of self, relationships, the world, and
even how you view God.

A template has been formed over years and now
paints a picture of how we see everything around us.
When we come to Christ our minds need to be renewed

because the world itself has created a template on how we should live and what the world considers to be in the range of normal.

We know that the Bible is the truth, and the world is forever moving away from the truth. In fact, it looks to desensitize people toward sin and normalize it. Therefore, we are not to be conformed to the ways of the world and need mind renewal.

Your view of self may be warped because you internalized the critical voice of your parents (graveclothes). Relationships may also be seen incorrectly, as the pain of the past may have caused mistrust or suspicion. A healthy view of yourself can be found in the Word of God and God wants to restore health to you and heal you of all your wounds.

Some may have chosen to believe a lie and therefore walk in darkness. Others have tunnel vision where their vision is limited. Yet some have rose-colored vision where they live in a make-believe world and some have optical illusions where they see things that are not there.

Whatever vision defect, God has new glasses for you. We must look into the true mirror. The mirror is the Word of God which will clearly show you your defects. The Word is clear that we must be careful as to what we entertain. We are told to bring every thought into captivity to the obedience of Christ (2 Corinthians 10:5).

Vain imaginations are to be cast down (2 Corinthians 10:5) and we are to meditate on that which is lovely, pure, and praiseworthy (Philippians 4:8).

We can also ask others to show us our blind spots. We all have them. There is safety in the multitude of counselors (Proverbs 11:14).

Questions to Consider:

1. Are you suspicious?
2. Are you overly critical?
3. Do you believe your past has helped create some of your trust issues?
4. Could you define what is a healthy identity?

9

Getting in My Own Way

Delight yourself also in the LORD, and He shall give
you the desires of your heart.
Psalm 37:4, NKJV

Many times, the enemy has been me! I have found myself getting in my own way. I would say the number one problem is our own *impatience*. Many people give up just before their breakthrough. We often allow frustration to get the upper hand, not considering the timing of God. "To everything *there is* a season, a time for every purpose under heaven" (Ecclesiastes 3:1 NKJV).

The question is, how are we perceiving the resistance? Are we seeing the roadblock as a stepping stone or a stumbling block? We may have an interpretation issue. Delays do not necessarily mean denial. Some things you are simply not ready for, or perhaps when you got the blessing you would forget about God.

Another roadblock may be insignificance or inferiority. Many do not see their value. This really is an identity problem. You are so valuable Christ laid down His life for you. Some people with deep-rooted feelings of insignificance exude arrogance or superiority to mask how they really feel about themselves. They are petrified to allow anybody to see it. People wear a lot of masks to cover up unwanted feelings.

Sometimes because of our pasts we feel very insecure. This is a confidence problem, and one may have a core shame-based problem. This means you are ashamed of yourself and afraid of being shamed again.

In the article, *Shame Excavation*, by Roth Rosenberg, he says, "The shame-based child becomes the adult 'human doing' who can never outrun their shame. There are two types of shame: shame for who you are and shame for what you have done. Shame for who you are is one's core shame."[37] Well, Jesus bore your shame on the cross. His people will never be put to shame and your sufficiency is of Christ not of yourself.

Another roadblock may be your own intellect. You may have a reasoning issue. This is when you come up with all the reasons why you cannot pursue a dream. Indecisiveness may be an issue and you are afraid to make decisions to move forward because of so many previous bad decisions. So, you make no decision for safety.

Others may have influenced you negatively through intimidation and shut you down. Anger is sometimes used by others to get you to back off. It is a form of control.

God wants to give you the desires of your heart, but I believe we need a real revelation of who we are as well as insight into our value and worth. I also believe evil company corrupts good character and it would be better to associate with those who will build us up and speak the truth in love.

Questions to Consider:

1. How do you perceive delays?
2. How do you respond to delays?
3. Is the Word of God a governing factor in your life?
4. Are you angry at God?

1 0

My Family is Dysfunctional

Christ has redeemed us from the curse of the law, having be-
come a curse for us (for it is written, "Cursed is everyone who
hangs on a tree"), that the blessing of Abraham might come
upon the Gentiles in Christ Jesus, that we might receive the
promise of the Spirit through faith.
Galatians 3:13-14, NKJV

If we study our Bibles, we can find quite a bit of dys-function. Abraham lied about his relationship with Sar-ah, calling her his sister. (Genesis 12:10-20, and Genesis 20). In Genesis 26:1-10 Isaac did the same thing calling Rebekah his sister.[38] What was taught? *Lying* is an ac-ceptable way to resolve conflict.

Other dysfunctional patterns can be seen with re-gard to attachment styles:

In each generation there was a pattern of a mother who was overinvested in the life of a son. Sarah was too involved with Isaac, Rebekah enmeshed with Jacob; and Rachel was totally involved only with Joseph. Three generations of mothers doting on their sons.[39]

I have seen families where the boys are always pampered, and the girls were forced to be strong and independent. The sin of favoritism will wreak havoc. We clearly see that in the life of Joseph and his brothers. However, "Joseph became the transitional person in the family lineage stopping the dysfunctional pattern in the fourth generation."[40]

Unhealthy sinful behaviors and patterns of interaction are learned generationally. If I were to go through your family line, it is most likely you will see reoccurring themes such as addiction, adultery, and divorce until someone in the family comes to know Christ. It is then that generational cycles are broken, as the individual appropriates the work of the cross.

If we were to view your family line and relationships over several generations, we would likely see family patterns tend to repeat themselves. By this, I mean how family members interact with one another. Sometimes the attachment is strong to the point of enmeshment. This means there is no clear boundary where one person ends and the other begins. This unhealthy attachment often hinders the development of self-governing and decision-making. The opposite style of attachment may be detachment or neglect.

Families will do anything to maintain homeostasis (balance) even if it is dysfunctional. They may even assign the role of scapegoat. This has to do with blame transference to get back in balance, to get back to the way things were. Families may also keep secrets and tell lies to maintain homeostasis.

The good news is Jesus can come in and restore all brokenness. His Word applied can transform our families. It takes only one family member submitted to Christ to break ungodly patterns in the family line.

Questions to Consider:

1. How did your family resolve conflict?
2. Was there a sense of happy closure after the conflict or just a lot of yelling?
3. Have there been family patterns passed down the generational line?
4. Has there been a transitional person in your family line?

11

I Am Always Frustrated

But let patience have its perfect work, that you may be perfect and complete, lacking nothing.
James 1:4, NKJV

Drama queens don't do well at handling delays or resolving conflict. Conflict resolution skills are learned early in childhood. Displays of anger may have been shown as an effective way to resolve disputes or Momma may have put on dramatic tears to get her way. In any event, the drama queen will use these learned skills to get her needs met. She will be in for a rude awakening when the world does not respond the way she thinks it should. She just might meet other drama queens after all.

Drama queens can get well if they adopt a biblical worldview regarding delays. God does not operate on our timetable. He lives by an eternal clock. His desire for our lives is different than our temporary carnal pleasures. God's motivation is love and wants it to be well with us. Hearing no or wait may be in our best interest.

Delay does not necessarily mean denial. There are some things we think we are ready for, but God knows we are not. "I still have many things to say to you, but you cannot bear them now" (John 16:12, NKJV).

Having to wait on some things may come to test obedience. God knows all things and your heart: He wants to show you what is in your heart. The real test is how you will act when things are not going your way.

Delay may come because God is working in someone else's heart that is close to you. Their life may be especially important to your destiny fulfillment or vice versa. It is not all about you.

God may "stretch your faith" and cause you to press into Him more. Many times, I have seen people get abundantly blessed and then forget God. The stretching will cause you to remember.

Many times, delays are used to work patience in us, but we must allow patience to have her perfect work. God is looking to develop the fruit of the spirit in your life. Twice-baked potatoes are better than instant mashed.

Delay comes and when God comes through, it is a mighty victory. The 11:59 God shows up and displays his glory to show Himself strong on your behalf. You will have a greater appreciation of the faithfulness of your God.

Many drama queens have *low frustration tolerance*. This simply means you want what you want when you want it and you want it without any trouble. We must remember who God is in our lives. Are we submitted to the sovereign rule of the Lord Jesus Christ? Do you believe our steps are ordered by Him and our times are in His hands? If so, we can be content whether abased or abound. We can overcome low frustration tolerance.

> Thus, we should not interpret divine delays as signs of divine reluctance. Delays are tools to perfect our faith. Christ is looking to find a tenacity in our faith that prevails despite delays and setbacks. He seeks to create a perseverance within us that outlasts the test of time, a resolve that grows stronger during delays. When the Father sees this quality of persistence in our faith, it so touches His heart that He grants "legal protection" to His people.[41]

Questions to Consider:

1. Are you frustrated easily?
2. What are some other things you can do when you feel frustration rising?
3. Are you a yeller?
4. Can you be verbally or emotionally abusive during times of frustration?

1 2

A Different Perspective on Brokenness

The Lord is near to those who have a broken heart,
and saves such as have a contrite spirit.
Psalm 34:18, NKJV

How one views or perceives the meaning of the trauma is particularly important and will be a determining factor in your healing. If you are continually rehearsing the hurt and cursing the perpetrator you are empowering the kingdom of darkness and giving the devil a foothold. You are feeding the drama queen. Your carnal mind is ruling and reigning and this only leads to death. To be spiritually-minded is life and peace (Romans 8:6).

What if we could look at brokenness brought on by trauma from a different perspective?

On his site, Hebrew 4 Christians, John Parsons gives various views on brokenness and brings some salient points. He states, "Brokenness is the means through which God performs some of his deepest work within our hearts and also God uses broken vessels in his service."[42] The fact is every one of us have been broken somewhere in our lives and God works with what He has. While He works with what He has, He loves us too much to continually see us in pain. Brokenness is often a means to draw us closer to God for our healing.

In 2014, I was in a near-fatal car accident. Not only that, I was going through another trial which left me emotionally capsized. Sometimes, my friends, breaking is necessary and comes at an exceptionally low point in your life. Just when you thought it could not get any lower, it drops down another level. I have to say though, this place has been my best place with God. I could hear Him clearly as He drew near to my broken heart.

First let me say, God is not a sadist nor is He tyrannical. Sometimes things need to die so new life can come forth and sometimes major shaking comes into our lives because we are going down a path of destruction. In any event, God never wastes a wound and your misery will be your ministry. You will be able to give the comfort you received from God to others and be an effective minister.

God may be dealing with some form of idolatry in your life. This simply means that something or someone else is on the receiving end of your devotion more than God. The idol may be controlling your life and influencing your decisions. This is dangerous because you are giving rulership over your life to someone or something else. Only Jesus is worthy of that spot. He alone shed His blood and died a criminal's death in your place. Not to mention that only He alone is pure and just. He has no impure motives and no self-seeking agenda. His motivations are love-based and He has your best interests at heart.

Sometimes we find ourselves in very unhealthy relationships. We are attracted to that which is familiar, or we may be trying to gain mastery over a past traumatic memory. In any event, God may allow the breaking of your heart because the relationship is not good for you and you do not know any better or even know how to get out of the web.

God sees your end from your beginning. He saw what you could not see. Many drama queens suffer from excessive controlling behaviors or codependency. Psych Central gives a wonderful definition of codependency: "Belonging to a dysfunctional one-sided relationship when one person relies on the other for meeting nearly all of their emotional and self-esteem needs. A core characteristic is the need for approval and a sense of identity from others."[43] Again, this need is to be met by God alone. He makes us accepted in the Beloved and our identity comes from Him. We are children of God and belong to the family of God. In these types of relationships, God is erased in favor of a person.

Many times, people will hold on to a lie rather than look at a horrible truth. However, God desires truth in the most inward parts and does not want His children walking in deception. Truth bombs can break our hearts but only then can healing can come. Truth dispels darkness and fantasy, and delusions need to be cast down.

Trials may come to bring down pride and self-reliance. It is the only way to get you to look up to God for your help. Brokenness helps usher in a change of heart and perhaps a change of direction. Apostle Paul needed to be kicked off his high horse and shown the right way.

Brokenness reveals to you your need for Jesus and the condition of your heart. Sometimes we can become so resistant and dull of hearing to the voice of the Spirit, God must break the hardened shell of our hearts. The life of God cannot be kept hidden behind a wall, but it is to be shone for others to see and glorify God.

Perhaps now we can look at brokenness from a different perspective. Instead of getting mad at God, we can give thanks. Instead of blaming others, we could look at the part we played in a particular problem. I think the key is to be open and pliable in the Master's hands. We are His workmanship, not a *piece of work*.

Questions to Consider:

1. Have there been experiences in your life that you feel have caused brokenness in you?
2. Are you codependent?
3. Are there any idols in your life that need to be cast down?
4. Do you believe your emotions are attached to your belief system?

1 3

Resilience

Who is this coming up from the wilderness,
leaning upon her beloved?
Song of Solomon 8:5, NKJV

Resilience is bouncing back from difficult times, or the ability to adapt after a crisis of some sort. I genuinely believe I have bounced back because I have leaned on Christ and have trusted in His promises. As I waited on Him, He renewed my strength. It is He who has made me an overcomer. I also believe I have overcome situations because of beautiful divine connections who have supported me along the way; the Aarons, the Hurrs, the Barnabus's, the Titus's, if you will.

As a Christian, I believe in the power of Christ but also believe there are things we need to do to cooperate with the Holy Spirit. I do not have an aversion to the study of human behavior and feel we can learn much from the years of study in the soulical realm. However, psychologists tend to leave the power of Christ out and only focus on what the individual can do to improve themselves. In other words, the focus is more on self-help.

As much as resilience involves "bouncing back" from these difficult experiences, it can also involve growth. We know that Job was tried and came forth as gold (see Job 23:10). Good questions to ask are: Did I grow through it? Did I learn how to help others?

I have bounced back from difficulties because I first sought the Kingdom and learned to roll my cares upon Him. I do this with confidence, as we are to approach the throne of grace with confidence to obtain mercy in time of need.

Roll Your Burden Unto the Lord

We can learn much from the animal kingdom. Job 12:7 tells us to ask the animals and they will teach us. So, I would like to look at the camel. Proverbs 16:3 instructs us, commit your works to the Lord and your thoughts shall be established. "The word commit is Galal Strong's #1556: to roll, roll down, roll away, remove. In this text, the reader is encouraged to roll his works into God's care. The picture is of a camel burdened with a heavy load, when the load is to be removed, the camel kneels down, tilts far to one side and the load rolls off."[44]

Camels travel many miles in extreme conditions. They can navigate through harsh sand storms and temperature changes. God has equipped them with everything they were created for. Camels have extra eyelids and eyelashes for protection against sand. They have specialized toes to keep them from sinking and humps to store fat.[45]

Knowing your purpose on the planet will help you with your bounce back. God has built in you a divine capacity to fulfill your purpose. You have been purposely designed and God has built some resilience in you.

Questions to Consider:

1. What are some things that have aided you in receiving a bounce back?
2. What are some of the things that hindered your bounce back?
3. Have you ever had a wilderness experience where you came out leaning on Jesus? What was it?
4. Have you matured through trials? In what way?

1 4

What is the Will of God for My Life?

However, when He, the Spirit of truth, has come,
He will guide you into all truth; for He will not speak on
His own authority, but whatever He hears He will speak;
and He will tell you things to come.
John 16:13, NKJV

It is God's will that you know the will of God. Scripture affirms this. "For this reason we also, since the day we heard it, do not cease to pray for you, and to ask that you may be filled with the knowledge of His will in all wisdom and spiritual understanding" (Colossians 1:9, NKJV).

Some do not want to know the will of God because they prefer their own will. Some will sabotage their God-ordained destinies. Sheri Zampelli gives some reasons in her book, *From Sabotage to Success*. She says they choose to believe they are not good enough, they choose to compare themselves to others, are afraid of rejection, or chronically need to be in control.[46]

An inaccurate view of your worth and identity may be keeping you from moving forward. Self-defeating attitudes and behaviors may be keeping you from fulfilling your destiny. Perhaps it is time to decide to not go around the same mountain again. Invite God to show you the truth about yourself and ask for the grace to readjust.

You may be reading right now and are not sure what is the perfect will of God for your life. Rest assured that God wants you to know His will for your life. He has a good plan for you (see Jeremiah 29:11) and desires that it be well with you.

If you want to determine the will of God let us look at some A's. The first is to *Acknowledge* him in all your ways and He shall direct your paths (Proverbs 3:6). The promise here is that God will bring direction if you acknowledge Him *in all your ways.*

The word "ways" (Hebrew derek) means a road, a course, or mode of action and the word "acknowledge" suggests an intimacy with God in prayer that conceives and births blessings and victories.[47] The word "direct" (yashar Strong's #3474) means to be straight, upright, pleasing, good. To make straight and right. God will straighten out the path of his devoted."[48]

So here is an example: Yes Lord, I am lacking motivation. Yes Lord I am afraid, I do not want to be laughed at. Yes Lord, I always felt Joyce Meyers is better. My ways need to be changed. I acknowledge that Your ways are higher than mine.

The second A is, *Ask* God; inquire of the Lord. If any lacks wisdom let him ask and God will give it liberally (see James 1:5). Did you know that God spoke to Moses face-to-face, even plainly and not in dark sayings? God wants to have a frank conversation with us as one has with a friend. David would inquire of the Lord and receive specific battle strategies that would lead to victory.

We need to *Allow* the peace of God to rule your heart.

> And let the peace (soul harmony which comes) from Christ rule (act as umpire continually) in your hearts [deciding and settling with finality all questions that arise in your minds, in that peaceful state] to which as [members of Christ's] one body you were also called [to live]. And be thankful (appreciative), [giving praise to God always].].
>
> Colossians 3:15, AMPC

NIV reads, "Let the peace of Christ rule in your hearts, since as members of one body you were called to peace. And be thankful." We need to allow the peace of God to be the umpire of our hearts. Peace should rule the believer's heart. God's peace should guide our choices.

The fourth A is to *Assess*. Look at your current situation and what you are planning to do. Ask the following: 1) Does what I am planning to do, align with the Word? 2) Will what I do take away from devotional time? 3) Will what I do line up with the previous prophecy I knew to be true? 4) Will it negatively impact my loved ones?

God's will carries with it an ability to get the job done: God's burden is light, and His yoke is easy (Matthew 11:30). Also, God will give you the will and the "to do" for His good pleasure (see Philippians 2:13).

We want the approval of God. So, the fifth A is Approval. By this I mean, look for the nod and smile of God on your endeavor. Look for confirmations. God's signature of approval often comes by two or three witnesses (see Matthew 18:16).

Finally, the last A is to *Act* on your assignment. If you do not receive a check in your spirit, proceed forward. God will be faithful to let you know if you are going the wrong way. Submit to His will.

Questions to Consider:

1. Have you ever resisted an assignment from God? Why do you think you may have done that?

2. Have you made major decisions without asking God first? What was the result?

3. Have you gone around the same mountain over and over?

4. How will you stop your self-defeating behaviors?

1 5

Embracing Change

To everything there is a season, a time for
every purpose under heaven.
Ecclesiastes 3:1, NKJV

God has a timetable for everything; know that your
time is in His hands. God works in time and seasons.
The Bible speaks of the fullness of time (Galatians
4:4), preappointed times (Acts17:26), due season (Gala-
tians.6:9), and working everything beautiful in its time
(Ecclesiastes 3:11).

God is the author of change. Daniel 2:21 tells us
He changes the times and seasons. We must embrace
change, take hold of it, and accept it. Do not resist it.
We know that Jonah resisted and encountered the
Lord's correction.

Many warriors God used in the Bible had to embrace
change. Hebrews 11:8 tells us, by faith Abraham obeyed
and went, not knowing where he was going. It was a

major upheaval for him and his family but sometimes God works like this and requires that we simply obey.

God does call his people out of places. Acts 13:4 tells us, "So, being sent out by the Holy Spirit, they [Barnabus and Saul] went" (NKJV). Rebekah left her home and went to be the wife of Isaac, without having met him (Genesis 24). Ruth left all she knew and clung to Naomi (Ruth 1). Isaiah said, "Here am I! Send me" (Isaiah 6:8, NKJV).

Life brings many transitions. In the natural, we go through developmental milestones. The baby sits up, the baby crawls, the baby walks, the child goes to school, and then the nest is empty. There are also spiritual milestones: salvation, water baptism, holy ghost baptism, perhaps ordination. Change is a part of life both in the spiritual and natural realms.

Sometimes people resist change, so the Lord must intervene. The brook dried up for Elijah (see 1 Kings 17:7). A whale had to be sent to swallow Jonah (see Jonah 1:17) and Paul after seeing a great light fell to the ground (see Acts 9:3-4). It is best to simply obey the Lord's directives.

How do I know if God wants to bring change?
1. The grace where you are will start to lift (extreme frustration or a deadness). Know that the cloud is beginning to move (see Numbers 9:17).

2. What was once a delight is now a burden. His yoke is easy, and burden is light (see Matthew 11:30). God's yoke for you is custom-made. It is when we take other people's yokes it becomes too heavy or you are not casting your cares upon the Lord (see 1 Peter 5:7).

3. A knowing in your spirit the season is changing for you. Your spirit will bear witness.

4. I personally feel an unsettling in my spirit; a divine frustration.

So why are so many of God's people so resistant to change?

Many people resist change and will only change when the pain of staying the same becomes greater than the possible pain in the future. Often, we must hate where we are or what we are doing to make a move.

It is not really that people do not want change but are concerned about the possible loss that the change may bring. They are afraid of losing what they had and knew. Luke 5:39 tells us, "And no one, having drunk old wine, immediately desires new; for he says, 'The old is better'" (NKJV).

People are sometimes afraid of loss of power. This was seen with the Pharisees who did not want the change that Jesus was bringing. It reshuffled the power. They would no longer be able to *lord over*.

There are life and death cycles for everything. Sometimes we keep things on life support longer than they should be. Some things need a DNR: do not resuscitate.

People will not really be open for change unless they can see an advantage or benefit.
There were 4 lepers in the Bible who decided to make a change.

> Now there were four men with leprosy at the entrance of the city gate. They said to each other, "Why stay here until we die? If we say, 'We'll go into the city'—the famine is there, and we will die. And if we stay here, we will die. So let's go over to the camp of the Arameans and surrender. If they spare us, we live; if they kill us, then we die.
>
> 2 Kings 7:3-4, NIV

They were motivated to make the change. *Motivation is a key to change.* I may have an idea or a dream but if I'm not motivated to implement it, it will not likely happen.

There is a thing called treatment resistance. This simply means the person is resisting receiving help or may have little motivation to make the changes needed. Treatment would include helping people look at and resolve their ambivalence. Ambivalence means feeling two ways about something. 1 Kings 18:21 asks, "How long will you falter between two opinions?" (NKJV). This can also be called double-minded.

A counselor would look at the motivational level to determine where they are in the Stages of Change Model by Prochaska and DiClemente.

The stages of change are as follows:

Precontemplation: unaware of a problem
Contemplation: debate whether they have a problem
Determination: ready to change their behavior
Action: begin the process of changing
Maintenance: maintaining change
Relapse: falling back to old behavior.[49]

Treatment would involve increasing awareness of their need to change. I have found that many people simply do not want to put the effort into making the change or really don't see the need for it. A good counselor will roll with the resistance and bring thought-provoking questions.

If the change is from God, you will not be able to fight against it, and why would we want to? He has our best interests at heart. He wants us to succeed, prosper, and be in good health.

Questions to Consider:

1. Are you resistant to change of any kind?
2. What do endings mean for you?
3. Is there something you have had some ambivalence about?
4. Have you ever had a time where God had to intervene to make you change? What was the event? How did it turn out?

1 6

Not a Drama Queen: Abigail and Biblical Conflict Resolution

Blessed are the peacemakers, for they will be
called sons of God.
Matthew 5:9, NKJV

The Bible is clear, whatever we do, must be done in love and glorify God. This applies in resolving conflict. Let us look at a woman named Abigail who had fancy conflict resolution skills.

In 1 Samuel 25, we see Nabal (a churlish man and evil in his doings) a rich fool who lacked judgment, and his wife Abigail (a woman of good understanding and beautiful) come on the scene. As the story goes, David and his men protected Nabal's men and sheep out in the field, David then sends men to Nabal's house to ask for some food and Nabal says, "Who is David that I should give food? He could be a runaway slave." When David heard the report, he wanted to kill Nabal. He felt Nabal repaid him evil for good.

Now there was a young man who went and told Abigail how David's men watched out over Nabal's servants and that harm was about to come to the house. Abigail's response to the situation is to be commended, as she circumvented disaster from coming to her household. She chose to walk in humility and be a peacemaker. She noticed an offense had come and quickly looked to resolve it.

In 1 Samuel 25:18 we see Abigail made haste and took bread, wine, sheep, grain, raisins, and figs and loaded the donkeys. Abigail brought what David wanted. She clothed herself with humility and looked to the interests of the entire household.

Abigail reminded David that he did not need to avenge himself as the Lord would fight his battle. God used her to help David see another perspective.

When we are so heated, we tend to move on emotion, not on God's Word. Not so with Abigail. She relied on the ways of God and brought God's counsel. David said to her, "Blessed is your advice and blessed are you, because you have kept me this day from coming to bloodshed and from avenging myself with my own hand" (1 Samuel 25:33, NKJV).

Abigail was quick to resolve the offense and looked to overcome evil with good. I believe she was a woman led by the Spirit of God and was aware of the ways of God. I also believe she was attuned to the voice of God. I am reminded of the Beatitudes where it is written, "Blessed are the poor in spirit, for theirs is the kingdom of heaven" (Matthew 5:3, NKJV). The poor in spirit recognize their need for God's grace. "Blessed are the meek, for they shall inherit the earth" (Matthew 5:5, NKJV). Meekness is not weakness but controlled strength. She was a woman with this type of strength.

Questions to Consider:

1. Have you ever been a Nabal—unable to forgive?

2. Would you have been brave enough to encounter David?

3. What do you think made Abigail a woman of influence?

4. Have you ever had to deal with a fool? How did you handle it?

5. Humility plays an important part of reconciliation. What are your thoughts?

17

Navigating Through Crises

That day when evening came, he said to his disciples, "Let us go over to the other side." Leaving the crowd behind, they took him along, just as he was, in the boat. There were also other boats with him. A furious squall came up, and the waves broke over the boat, so that it was nearly swamped. Jesus was in the stern, sleeping on a cushion. The disciples woke him and said to him, "Teacher, don't you care if we drown?" He got up, rebuked the wind and said to the waves, "Quiet! Be still!" Then the wind died down and it was completely calm. He said to his disciples, "Why are you so afraid? Do you still have no faith?" They were terrified and asked each other, "Who is this? Even the wind and the waves obey him!"
Mark 4:35-41, NIV

The disciples were in a crisis. *Merriam-Webster* defines crisis as a crucial time, a turning point in the course of anything. Crises are turning points where people can possibly move toward growth. Crisis happens in everyone's life. But have you noticed that some handle crisis better than others? How one handles a crisis may have to do with perception of the threat, how much support they receive through it, and the coping skills that were developed in childhood.

Most people who are in crisis feel like it will last forever. Research shows that a crisis ends, and balance is restored within a maximum of six weeks. The trial does have an expiration date on it and God controls the thermostat (how hot it gets).

Everyone will encounter a crisis at some time in their life. In this world you will have tribulations (see John 16:33). Many get disillusioned when storms come and begin to ask God why He is not rescuing them. Many get mad and pull away from God. Their attitude says, *I will show you Lord...* A question most asked during tumultuous times is, where are you God when I am so overwhelmed?

After losing everything Job did not react with anger but instead said, "Oh that I knew where I might find Him that I might come to His seat!" (Job 23:3, NKJV). I want to remind you today that God is near even in the silence and we can approach the throne of grace with confidence knowing He is a God who hears.

In our opening text, we find what many of us do when going through hard times. We ask, God don't you love me? Have you left me? How long Lord? The disciples did not believe in their hearts that God was going to help them. How solidified were they in the fact that God was their helper? This foundational truth in many of us needs to be shored up. Their faith level in believing God "as helper" was *low*. How quickly they had forgotten their God was a miracle-working God.

When navigating the storm do not forget how God has continually helped you in the past. He is Jehovah Ezer: The Lord My Help.

Ebenezer

Ebenezer is derived from two words, eben or stone, and ezer or help, and thus means "stone of help". Samuel took a stone (eben) and set it between Mizpah and Shen and named it Ebenezer (literally "Stone of Help"), saying, "Thus far Jehovah has helped us." (1 Samuel 7:12).⁵⁰ During the heat of battle, we forget the faithfulness of God. It is a good time to remember how God has consistently delivered you time and time again.

Many look for other alternatives rather than wait on God for their help. Do not always look to jump out of the boat. The solution or answer may be close by or right next to you. The children of Israel looked to run back to Egypt when they encountered bitter waters at Marah. God had the solution. Moses simply needed to throw a stick in the water and guess what? It was made sweet to drink (see Exodus15).

Some people believe if everything is not going smooth or perfect, they are not in God's will. This is not true. God uses storms to get you to the other side. In other words, God uses difficult circumstances to mature you and get you where you need to be. I realize there are times when we need to jump ship, so to speak, but let it be what the Lord wants for your life. Acknowledge Him in all your ways and He will direct your steps.

Watch your declarations when in the storm. David said, "I lift up my eyes to the mountains—where does my help come from? My help comes from the Lord, the Maker of heaven and earth" (Psalm 121:1-2, NIV). Notice his declaration is different than, Lord are you sleeping?

Caleb, in the face of giants, said we are well able to overcome. In Numbers 13:30, Caleb told the people to be quiet and listen to Moses. Caleb said, "Let us go now and take possession of the land." Then Caleb stilled the people before Moses, and said, "Let us go up at once and possess it; for we are well able to overcome it." He believed what God said. He believed the report of the Lord.

Caleb is the one with a different spirit, as he wholeheartedly sought the Lord and knew God would keep His promise. Notice his declaration: We are well able to overcome, not, God have you left me?

Both David and Caleb were fully persuaded in whom they believed. They saw the circumstances but chose to believe God. They did not perceive the giants as an obstacle but rather something to overcome. Caleb called his enemies bread for him.

What is your perspective? Is it faith-based or fearbased? Is it positive or negative? How do you perceive the storm and what are you declaring in the storm?

I realize that some storms shake us to the core. God will shake all which can be shaken. It has been my personal experience that whenever God shook me to the core, He was dealing with idols in my life. I was dependent on something or someone other than God. The greatest revelations or aha moments have come to me through a storm. Sometimes we can blindly walk or deceive ourselves. It takes a storm to shake us out of disillusionment. Many a truth is revealed in a storm. Our attitudes are made plain and the hearts of others may be exposed to you as well.

Storms help build spiritual muscles. You remember David who said the same God who delivered from the paw of the lion and the bear will deliver me from the uncircumcised Philistine? (see 1 Samuel 17:37). Many Christians are flabby spiritually, as they never put their faith into action.

Some storms are only booms in the sky. They seem scary at first but then they roll in and roll right out without any negative impact. The enemy is just trying to create fear but God has not given us a spirit of fear, but of power and of love and of a sound mind (2 Tim.2:17, NKJV). We as Christians can take comfort in knowing that in every storm God is in the boat with us.

We do want to be careful of impulsivity when in the midst of the storm. I personally have made poor decisions because I acted on impulse. Impulsivity exalts folly (Proverbs 14:29). It is a good idea to seek the counsel of the Lord and perhaps ask God what He may be trying to teach you through the storm. Finally, recall past victories and trust in the God who loves you more than you will ever be able to comprehend.

Questions to Consider:

1. Have you found yourself asking, God where are you in the storms?
2. What does silence from God mean to you?
3. Do you look to run away when times get tough?
4. Do you withdraw from God in crisis?
5. What are some coping skills you can use to help get you through to the other side?

1 8

Treatment for Trauma

For I am the Lord who heals you.
Exodus 15:26, NKJV

There are various treatments for trauma that depend not only on the type of trauma but the severity and length of traumatic events. Also, of important consideration is whether a mental health disorder is now present due to that trauma and what the impact is on everyday functioning. Some may have Post-Traumatic Stress Disorder (PTSD), Generalized Anxiety Disorder (GAD), or Major Depressive Disorder (MDD), and a clinician will treat accordingly. While this is not a book on the treatment of trauma, know there is a great deal of professional help out there with proven success using evidence-based treatments. Beware of wacky stuff out there given by people who do not know what they are doing.

Some treatments will not sit well or fit the Christian belief system. It is important that you find a counselor who has an understanding of the renewed mind of the Christian and sensitivity to Christian culture. For example, many Christians will not meditate on anything other than the Word. They will not participate in guided imagery or utilize mantras for relaxation. They will not empty their minds or stare into someone else's eyes to create a oneness bond. Also, many Christians will not practice yoga due to its original roots. The Christian's happy place is Jesus. A secular therapist may or may not know this.

I want to promote the healing power of the Lord Jesus Christ, as I personally can attest to His delivering power. He wants to heal us of all our wounds and restore health to us. He will often show you treasures about yourself that you are unaware of. He may even uncover past pain you have suppressed. He reveals to heal. The Holy Spirit who knows all things can bring revelation in a certain area that can quickly set you free.

Please keep in mind, doctors may be the stream of healing God chooses to use. Sometimes a professional is needed to help you walk through some very traumatic memories and sometimes medication is needed to treat. You may not agree with me on this matter but if you have ever seen someone suffer from severe depression or mania, you just might have a change of mind. A good counselor should be able to determine the right course of action for each individual.

Conclusion

Hopefully after reading this book you may have some more empathy for the drama queen, or at least some greater understanding of her behaviors. If you are the drama queen reading this book, hopefully you learned something about why you may do the things you do.

At the end of the chapters, questions were asked to stimulate introspection. They can also be used in a group setting to validate feelings and normalize experiences. Further, members of the group can share their testimonies and empower each other. They overcome by the blood of the Lamb and the word of their testimony (see Revelation 12:11).

May we all be the soothing balm to those who are hurting. Let us treat all with respect and if we must establish healthier boundaries, let us do so. As an ambassador of the Kingdom, I want to be showing the character of our King of Glory: the Lord Jesus Christ.

Jesus was meek and lowly at heart. He was an extender of mercy and grace. He did not retaliate but overcame evil with good. My prayer is that we represent Jesus here on the earth and be vessels of honor, fit for the Master's use.

If you have never invited Jesus to be your personal Lord and Savior, please pray:

Father, I am a sinner in need of forgiveness. I believe Jesus died on the cross for my sins and rose from the dead. He is the only acceptable sacrifice for my sins. Lord Jesus come into my heart. I believe you are the Lord who died on the cross, was buried, and rose again. Thank you, Jesus, for dying for my sins. Govern my life.

If you prayed this prayer, welcome to the family of God. Find a Bible-believing spirit-filled church and grow in the grace and knowledge of the Lord Jesus Christ.

Bibliography

Bulman, Ronnie Janoff. *Shattered Assumptions: Toward a New Psychology of Trauma*. NY, NY: Free Press, 1997.

Burgo, Joseph. *Why Do I do That?* Chapel, Hill, NC: New Rise Press, 2012.

Carnes, Patrick. *The Betrayal Bond: Breaking Free of Exploitive Relationships*. Deerfield Beach, Fl: Health Communications, Inc. 1997.

Clinton, Timothy & Gary Sibcy. *Attachments*. Brentwood, TN: Integrity Publishers, 2002.

_____& George Ohlschlager. *Competent Christian Counseling*. Colorado Springs, CO: Waterbrook Press, 2002.

Gray, Enod. *Neglect the Silent Abuser: How to Recognize and Heal from Childhood Neglect*. Enod Gray, 2018.

Gibson, Lindsay. *Adult Children of Emotionally Immature Parents: How to Heal from Distant, Rejecting or Self Involved Parents*. Oakland, CA: New Harbinger Productions, 2015.

Hayford, Jack. *New Spirit-Filled Life Bible*. Nashville, TN: Thomas Nelson Inc., 2002.

Herman, Judith. *Trauma and Recovery: The Aftermath of Violence from Domestic Abuse to Political Terror*. NY, NY: Basic Books, 1997.

McCloud, Casper. *Exposing the Spirit of Self Pity*. Mt. Aukum, CA: Life Application Ministries Publications, 2012.

Mellody, Pia. *Facing Love Addiction*. NY, NY: HarperCollins Publishers, 2003.

Russoti, James. *Understanding the Impact of Trauma*, 2019.

_____. *Trauma Awareness*, 2019.

Sanderson, Christine. *Counselling Adult Survivors of Child Sexual Abuse*. 3r ed. Philadelphia, PA: Jessica Kingsley Publishers, 2002.

Streep, Peg. *Daughter Detox: Recovery for an Unloving Mother and Reclaiming Your Life*. NY NY: ileDespoir Press, 2017.

Webb, Jonice & Christine Musello. *Running on Empty*. NY, NY: Morgan James Publishing, 2019.

Zampelli, Sheri. *From Sabotage to Success: How to Overcome Self Defeating Behaviors and Reach Your True Potential*. Lincoln NE: iUniverse Inc., 2006.

Articles and Web

Frangipane, Francis. "Legal Protection" Identitynetwork.net

Parsons, John. Nishberi Lev. Hebrew4Christians.com 12/12/10.

Prochaski &DiClimente Stages of Change of Model. Stepuprogram.org

Rosenberg, Russ. Shame Excavation: Unearthing Toxic Shame. Huffpost.com 1/23/2014.

Smith, Ann. How to Break the Patterns of Love Addiction. Psychology Today.com Dec. 1,2010.

"Acting Out" Healthline.com/health/acting out.

Body Dysmorphic Disorder. WebMD, Mental Health. www.webmd.com 2020.

Camel Facts. Soft Schools.com

Jehovah Ezer: The Lord my Help. Preceptaustin.org, 8/22/2016.

Nine Devastating Effects of the Absent Father. The Father Code, 6/24/2015.

Symptoms of Codependency. Psychcentral.com

What is a love addiction? Psychcentral.com

About the Author

Dr. April Griseta is a Doctor of Ministry as well as a national conference speaker. Among her accomplishments are the establishing of a local church, hosting CTN Clearwater's TV show "Bounce Back", and obtaining a license in mental health counseling. Dr. A has been active in church ministry for nearly thirty years.

Endnotes

1 Patrick Carnes, *The Betrayal Bond: Breaking Free of Exploitive Relationships* (Deerfield Beach, FL: Health Communications, Inc., 1997), 26.

2 Acting Out". https://healthline.com/health/acting-out. Accessed 12/27/2020.

3 Justin Russoti. Understanding the impact of trauma. Modified chapter 3 of Trauma Informed Care in Behavioral Health Services; Treatment Improvement Protocol ((TIP) Series 57 by Substance Abuse and mental Health Services Administration published in 2014. Modified in 2019.

4 Justin Russoti. Trauma Awareness. Modified Chapter 2 of Trauma Informed Care in Behavioral Health Services: Treatment Improvement Protocol (TIP) Series 57 by Substance Abuse and Mental health Services Administration published in 2014. Modified in 2019.

5 Ibid.

6 Judith Herman, *Trauma and Recovery: The Aftermath of Violence from Domestic Abuse to Political Terror* (New York; Basic Books, 1992),56.

7 Ronnie Janoff-Bulman, *Shattered Assumptions: Toward a New Psychology of Trauma* (New York, NY:

Free Press, 1992),7.

8   Enod Gray, *Neglect the Silent Abuser: How to Recognize and Heal from Childhood Neglect* (Self published, 2018), 36-37.

9   ustin Rossoti (2019). Understanding the Impact of Trauma. Modified chapter 3 of Trauma Informed Care in Behavioral Health Services: Treatment Improvement Protocol (IP) Series 57 by Substance Abuse and Mental Health Services Administration (SAMHSA) published in 2014. Table 1: Immediate and Delayed Reactions to Trauma.

10 Christine Sanderson, *Counselling Adult Survivors of Sexual Abuse third edition* (Phil., PA: Jessica Kingsley Publishers,2006), 55.
    • Italics in parenthesis are mine.

11 Sanderson, *Counselling Adult Survivors of Sexual Abuse third edition* ,44.

12 Ibid., 92.
    • Italics in parenthesis are mine.

13 Sanderson, *Counselling Adult Survivors of Sexual Abuse third edition.*, 71.

14 Ibid., 93.

15 Janice Webb & Christine Musello. *Running on Empty* (New York, NY: Morgan James Publishing,2019), 4.

16 Endo Gray. Neglect *The Silent Abuser: How to recognize and Heal from Childhood Neglect* (Self-Published, 2018), 81.

17 Lindsay C. Gibson. *Adult Children of Emotionally Immature Parents: How to Heal from Distant, Rejecting or Self-involved Parents.* New Harbinger Productions: Oakland, CA,2015), 11.

18 Ibid., 19-20.

19 Peg Streep, *Daughter Detox: Recovering from an Unlov-*

ing Mother and Reclaiming Your Life (New York, NY: Ile D'Espoir Press, 2017), .35-37.

20 Jonice Webb, Christine Musello, *Running on Empty: Overcome Your Childhood Emotional Neglect* (New York, NY: Morgan James Publishing,2019), 5.

21 Dr. Tim Clinton & Dr. Gary Sibcy. *Attachments: Why you Love, Feel, and Act the Way you Do* (Brentwood, TN: Integrity Publishers, 2002), 35.

22 Ibid., 36.

23 Joseph Burgo, *Why do I do That?* (Chapel Hill, NC: New Rise Press, 2012), 7.

24 Ibid., 10.

25 Ibid., 15.

26 Ibid., 65-160.

27 Burgo, *Why do I do that?*, 164.

28 Ibid., 165.

29 Ibid., 168.

30 Casper McCloud *Exposing the Spirit of Self-Pity* (Mt. Aukum, CA: Life Application Ministries Publications, 2012), 5.

31 Ibid., 9.

32 The Nine devastating effects of the absent father. The Father Code. Jun 24,2015.

33 Web MD. Mental Health: Body Dysmorphic Disorder. www.webmd.com. June 30, 2020.

34 Pia Mellody. *Facing Love Addiction* (NY, NY: Harper-Collins Publishers, 2003), xi.

35 Psychcentral.com/blog. What is love Addiction?

36 Ann Smith. "How to break the pattern of Love addiction" *Psychology Today*, Dec. 1,2010.

37 Ross Rosenberg "Shame Excavation: Unearthing Toxic Shame": huffpost.com/entry/shame. 1/23/2014.

38 Timothy Clinton & George Ohlschlager. *Competent Christian Counseling. Volume One* (Colorado Springs: CO, Waterbrook Press, 2002), 533.

39 Ibid., 533.

40 Ibid., 534

41 Francis Frangipane:" Legal Protection", Identitynetwork.net Accessed 12/24/2020.

42 John Parsons. Nishberi Lev. Hebrews for Christians.com Dec 11, 2010.

43 Symptoms of Codependency.Psychcentral.com Accessed 12/28/2020.

44 Jack Hayford. *Spirit-Filled Bible* (Nashville, TN: Thomas Nelson, Inc. 2002), 821.

45 Adapted from Camel facts, Softschools.com

46 Sheri Zampelli. *From Sabotage to Success: How to Overcome Self Defeating Behavior and Reach your True Potential* (Lincoln NE: iUniverse Inc., 2006), 18-27.

47 Jack Hayford. *New Spirit-Filled Life Bible.*(Nashville, TN: Thomas Nelson, Inc. 2002),807.

48 Ibid., 807.

49 Progchaska & Di Climentes Stages of Change Model. Stepupprogram.org/docs/handouts/step up_Stages_of_Change_pdf

50 Preceptaustin.org. Jehovah Ezer The Lord My help.8/22/2016.